AMERICAN URN

AMERICAN URN

Selected Poems
(1987-2014)

Mark Irwin

THE ASHLAND POETRY PRESS

Printed in the United States of America
ISBN: 978-0-912592-94-7
Library of Congress Control Number: 2014935201

Cover art by Jill Hadley Hooper: *Fireflies*, 2006
Cover design by Jonathan Weinert
Author photo by Steve Cohn / University of Southern California

"Buffalo Nickel," "Vista," "The Juvescence of Autumn," "Tomato Soup," "White," "Orpheus," "Warhol," "Woolworth's," "Grand Canyon," "History's Pause," "The Face," "Robert Mapplethorpe's Photograph of Apollo, 1989," and "Heart" from *Quick, Now, Always*. Copyright © 1996 by Mark Irwin. "White City," "No Continuing City," "Horse," "Mansion of Happiness," "X," "Discovery," "Even Now," "Anatomy," "Serious Earth," "These Cars," "Autumnal," "Buffalo," "The Sheer Weight of History," and "Sparrow" from *White City*. Copyright © 2000 by Mark Irwin. "Once," "A Glass of Water," "Go," "Passing," "An Autumn Essay," "Water," "Because," "Rodeo," "Before Us," "Potter's Field," "My Father's Hats," "Poem," "Vermeer," and "It's True" from *Bright Hunger*. Copyright © 2004 by Mark Irwin. All reprinted with the permission of The Permissions Company, Inc. on behalf of BOA Editions Ltd., www.boaeditions.org.

"The Wisdom of the Body," "Point Nine," "Point Eight," "Point Five," "Point Four," "Point Three," and "Point Two" from *Against the Meanwhile* © 1988 by Mark Irwin. Reprinted by permission of Wesleyan University Press, www.wesleyan.edu/wespress.

Large White House Speaking, New Issues Press, Western Michigan University, 2013
Tall If, New Issues Press, Western Michigan University, 2008
Bright Hunger, BOA Editions, Rochester, NY, 2004
White City, BOA Editions, Rochester, NY, 2000
Quick, Now, Always, BOA Editions, Rochester, NY, 1996
Against the Meanwhile (3 Elegies), Wesleyan University Press, 1989
The Halo of Desire, Galileo Press, Baltimore, MD, 1987

for Lisa Utrata and Mary Lou Irwin

Acknowledgments

Poems from the first six books appeared in the following journals. Many thanks to those editors:

AGNI Review, American Letters & Commentary, American Poetry Review, The Atlantic Monthly, Boston Review, Chelsea, Colorado Review, Conjunctions, Denver Quarterly, FIELD, The Georgia Review, Gulf Coast, Hotel Amerika, Hunger Mountain, Interim, Iowa Review, The Journal, Kenyon Review, Laurel Review, Luna, Massachusetts Review, Mid-American Review, The Nation, New England Review, New Letters, New Ohio Review, The New Republic, The Ohio Review, Orion, The Paris Review, Pequod, Poetry (Chicago), Shenandoah, Smartish Pace, Subtropics, Tri-Quarterly, Western Humanities Review, Willow Springs, Volt.

"Robert Mapplethorpe's Photograph of Apollo (1988)" appeared as a *Pushcart Prize Selection, volume XIX.*

"Autumnal" appeared as a *Pushcart Prize Selection, volume XXIII.*

"When I Died" was reprinted as a *Pushcart Prize Selection, volume XXVIII.*

"Elegy (with Advertisement) Struggling to Find its Hero" was reprinted as a *Pushcart Prize Selection, volume XXXI.*

"The Irises" was reprinted in *Western Wind*, 5th edition, McGraw Hill, 2005.

"Ends," "Ghost," "Stopping by the River in Spring," and "The Death" were featured and reprinted electronically on Poetry Daily.

Contents

II. *Tall If* (2008)

III. *Bright Hunger* (2004)

IV. *White City* (2000)

V. *Quick, Now, Always* (1996)

VI. *Against the Meanwhile* (1988)

VII. *The Halo of Desire* (1987)

I.

Large White House Speaking (2013)

Ghost

Now your name's just a guest here, one that cancels
all hellos. Fleshless
you come & go through the mansion

of air. How
will I address you, small
weather? Sometimes your name's

a dress like an iron
bell the years
swing shadows from

longer than home. Can you hear
that word peal? I'm going
there now,

carrying the windows
from inside
all the vowels.

Red Feather

This red feather floating down
from the canopy of a tree, the one
we watch all of our lives, then remember
as so many other breathing

things. Caught in a jar, the tadpoles slowly
lost their gills and tails to become
fat, knuckley, green. What

future tense to describe them
then? What grammar
I still look for

dissolving
in a dissolving
past. The owl

blinks its glass eyes
in a tree. Sometimes I think the red feather's
the word *is*. I crack the skull

of an egg and watch the albumen
whiten in a hot
pan. Look, someone's carrying red feathers

into a church where they grow into
a choir of blowing
mouths. My father once said

that all of our lives
we travel between the towns
of *yes* and *no.* I hesitated, smiled,

then walked into a sun-ripe
woods. *Red feather red
feather,* we enter

bodies then place
them into the earth or
flame. April now

and the frogs crawl up
through the mud
to sing.

When I See This X-Ray of a Hand's

long, jointed bones, floating like a bird's, prehistoric, knuckling

in their brightness, as if to perform some magic trick, to pull

a kerchief from the debut of darkness, I feel dangerous

as a spy, though unwilling as that reach toward something

between milk and sorrow, yet a gift, though be it

a knife, slow like time's, then I feel myself straining, listening

to the long echo of flesh say *hello*.

Rider

As I carried my mother from the hospital bed
across the room toward the chair by the window,
she played with my gold watch as if it were a toy,
flipping the strap up and down, then singing *Giddyup,*
Giddyup, but as I looked at her she did not smile
so I nodded my head, snorted, then put a pencil
in my mouth, as bit, and cantered about the room
till I was out of breath, puffing, and she patted me, saying,
Good boy, Good boy, so I pawed the carpet, slobbering a little
like her, as she waved and I nodded my mane,
until this was how we said goodbye one spring
while the sun shrank to a white hot BB among a thousand
others receding in the jeweled, black sky as the rivers
galloped away with her breath through the dark green land.

Empire

He wore a little spiraled hat and wrote a song
that everyone sang. He lived on the mountainside
above a lake with a mythical beast he'd subdued.
A train circled the village each hour, over and over,
as he leaned down over the clock of his world
where people were days becoming months and years.
In a park, from the hides of ten cows, he'd constructed
a giant ball that everyone touched until it became
a torn rag. He had no family, and because he worried
so much about them: *What if, what if, what if,* like another
beast pawing away, he'd invented a pill for everyone
old that allowed you to continue slowly to grow
until you forgot everything you once knew.

What You Might Say of Christ

At the junction between Gnat and God he came from Grief
to make a city named Marvel. The Milk-

words he spoke turned adults
to children, their Minds vivid as with the scent

of bananas. Beyond body, trees ushered dusk purples fast and silent: Censers
gilded through Centuries like the immensity
of a Minute

wherein the Bee trundles
from the pollen-crowned Stamen against the spathe's
white arena.

The Death

of death, is that not
what we want? For a moment to foil it
with flushed skin in the mud
house, or with a word
wounding the air, such that others stand around

surprised and forgetful. *Now*
is not a time, but all times, each word says.
In the perfect, long past
world, cells cloned really lived
forever, for though they died, all

were the same. In a coma
he looked like a sleeping child. I pulled a comb
through his hair, and think of it
now, pausing, placing

a comma. Left
with words what do you build? Something
green, a kind of pier to walk out on?
Angela showed me

three black Lab fetuses taken from
a spay. In a test tube
you could see their heads: the protoplasmic dot
of each dark nose
chasing ducks through the snow.

Elegy

I carry a ball and glove. I study the stars. I arrive and depart.
"Love many, lose some till none remain," the sailor sang. Ho Hum.
Near dusk the shadows of humans resemble stones. Inside
the house we are suddenly weightless, having not seen
each other for years, then touch like lights rehearsing the latitudes
of our names. Once in the bracken I did find myself looking for
a blown hat, now I'm polishing the lens of a telescope to make
the distant more bright. We had a girl pink as a shrimp. Her
birth wail filled our gaze that grew and grew till seeing burst
a second's glory. We're still proud, but her dolls get older. The colossi
of two pop stars flash on a giant screen. We gaze up like ancients not
privy. Time's a game of catch and pitch. On ships I think of
barns, in sleep I sail the land. I like green best when it courses
like fire.—A glove, a ball, a house collapsed. A carcass of vowels wept.

Hungry

I'm hungry for the leaves, their ochre and blaze, hungry
for their evening and the sun's
hammer. Hungry
for the dusk filled with musty scent of apple and grape, hungry for the trill
of crickets, and for the first stars. So hungry
I drive a stake into the ground
for each one and grow
hungrier as it grows
darker. I'm hungry for the constellations, for that one striding like an ichthyosaur
across the night sky. Hungry
for the pitch-black above that reminds me of words,
their names for things beyond what they are,
and for the feelings they carry on which I gorge.

Church Engine

Speech crumbling through emotion, this hole
we tear in the world with our bodies. We could see tomorrow's
infant-reaching hands. What can be known,
really? The way you
push me up and pull me down
from sleep. —Bone, muscle, fascia, skin. We tried to write
what we heard. No one
was speaking. —Drone of radio, TV. Are you
connected? By a stoplight, a man
on his knees. "Please," he said. Behind that word
a shelf, then nothing. Cars
leaving the walls of a city. Without
a map, we begin
singing.

Poem Beginning with a Line by Milosz

"The most beautiful bodies are like transparent glass."
They are bodies of the selfless or of those newly
dead. What appears transparent is really flame
burning so brightly it appears like glass. What
you're looking through is the act of giving: One
thing in life needed desperately, given to another,
or perhaps life itself. The most beautiful bodies
are not transparent, but sometimes the color
of lead, like the elephant whom a child with some
peanuts lifts by the trunk in his hand in the swirling
dust, so that it appears he has lifted a monument
or a city with all its pain. The bodies that seem
transparent are made of an ice so pure it appears
to be glass sweating, where you, desiring another,
glimpse your own face that weighs nothing and is burning.

Creation

The green archipelago
of spots, dark mottled, cast on a trout's back, each
one a terra nova, reef around which you might swim, cutting your hands,
or the gold sparks from the miner's pick axe, semen
of Christ. The ape, safely aware of humans, meticulously
picks seeds from grapes, fussy like us, while
beneath cumuli scudding low, sphered
dandelions dissolve. Why
you jumped I'll never know, but enjoy the way
wind catches their carved heads. Originality
in extremis: their seeds a syntax rivering, pausing, negotiating
eddies of feeling. Memory is love's quarry, where the word
once stung, its verb become mansioned
noun. That kiss now a fossil.

In Winter,

I like to walk out of the house in evening
when the bronze light's cast rose and people seem
made all of a liquid and I can walk right through them.
There's Wilda now, sweeping leaves from the sidewalk.
Five years ago she lost her husband Wayne,
who once on a picnic table unfolded a National Park map
and traced, with mustard on his finger, the route
his Jeep took. She holds the broom as if it were a child,
close to her chest, and *sweeps, sweeps*. And there's Luella
by the picture window, in a white sweater in front of her white house
throwing salt on the porch. Months after Nathan died on a bed
in the living room, I helped her hang sheets on the line
one warm April day. We stood within lofting walls
in strict sunlight, and for a moment accidentally touched,
as if to get our bearings in the new, loose wind pushing up so much glare.

On Sunday, Sometimes,

I'll start in late afternoon and follow the words of a new sentence
until evening finds their appropriate dusk, then squinting, rapt
with the moment, I'll open the photo album and descend
into its cellar, where people are walking toward me, out from
the white chancel of each picture, behind which a mountain
looms, all of its snow melting. They are sloshing through twilight
now, their hands dripping, pointing toward my mouth, walking
on the road of my sentence that now smells of fresh tar in the summer
heat, and for a moment their cheeks flush, and the frayed threads
of their clothes ravel into one truth, and from the building and shadowed
cumuli, lightning pins the quick of a greening world with the babble
of every word, their fingers like mice, thirsty, scurrying across my face.

Of the Body,

I know only its want, veering like a swallow
through dusk, but what
of our sleep, where like a flame's tuft we
change, grow, dissolve. Asylum
beyond pink flesh where all
the words have gills, wings. *What sayst you*
when those gone have ears like drums,
sails? I courted infinity like a ghost, still
half in love with earth, just to call the dead back
for a moment, in a panic of light,
and they stood there in the grass, each of its green lances
where I was a boy riding, writing the feelings down
for which there are no words, writing them with a brightness
by which it is impossible to read.

Large White House Speaking

—From morning to evening the resolution of light through windows.
We would like to, *yes*. We would like to go. We would like to stay,
but friends are calling, summoning, waving. It's a man, woman,
child. It's a man, woman, boy. It's a man, woman, young man.
Hi, how are you? Yes, I'm fine, thank you. There's a dog,
sofa, tables, chairs, ottoman, books, records, toys, pictures. A house
is a pocket with many smaller pockets: rooms, closets, drawers. You
are reaching now into the darkness. From morning to evening
the resolution of light's the resolution of time. People are windows,
lenses that focus emotion the way a magnifying glass focuses
light, and the bright points burst into flame, from morning to memory.
Yes, we would like to, yes. We would like to, *yes,* summon them
back, then love is that distance magnified by darkness. Why is it when
I say *now* you do not get closer, but shine like something smashed,
luminous and ringing as the space grows larger. I remember when the back
of his head fit snuggly in my palm from morning till evening, *yes, we would
like to, yes.* Then it was hard to—*yes*—think of the distance from God.

The Cake

One spring when we were children she placed the red cake
on the table. *What kind is it?* we asked. *Cherry,* she said, but we had
never seen frosting that red. More red than tulips, more red than her lipstick
or nails. It was a holiday and we were all very hungry, but when she set
it on the table my father went mad, rubbing the frosting all over his face
then babbling like a clown. My sister stood on her chair and began crowing
like a rooster. Our dog snarled at it, then ran outside in circles
before collapsing on the grass. I remember dreaming of barns, hundreds of them
all filled with yellow hay. Finally we all ate. We ate
it ravenously in big handfuls, stuffing it into our mouths, but the more we ate
the more of it remained, while mother watched, laughing, never
laughing so loud. Then we all went outside and stood on the green
lawn. We are standing there now as the sun comes out and the snow
begins falling and the swallows curve and glide around that cake's steep walls.

II.

Tall If (2008)

Tall If

It had something to do with the flowers, their brief tents
and ballast of color, and with the pollen
spilled like gold sugar onto the lawn.

It had something to do with each of our
lives, when we stood between evening
and forever, and someone

spoke and the words made a kind of grass
all over the white page. We
waited there, picnicking

in that brief summer. Yesterday I planted
the seeds, and today their fire
leafs, climbs. I will

water the fire till the fire greens
between red sky and blue
earth. Fool,

this is the way time
works. One minute the salt
becomes sugar, or the flesh you

held becomes distant as cloud, or slow
and perfect as stone. —Privileged
moments when the light

comes out of the air and stands unused
for a while. And so we walked
out of our minds

into the sky, ignorant of each gesture
calling us back, the glittering
armor on the ground.

Voice, Distant, Still Assembling

Walking farther there, I am glad we
       age slowly, discovering now in memory
  similar frontiers of a physical world, visiting
as though for the first time
       ruins of a once great city, yet novel

       in the crumbling light. We trip
and stumble, unaware, youthful in the obscurity
  of shadow, a kind of spring
in itself. *Itself,* where I touch places, gone, often
       confused to find a new home
not torn and built of green, but of a crumbling

orange, and *there, there,* as though walking
       through fire, taking pleasure in the fleeting
walls and lingering agoras, I glimpse
  ghost bodies and caress the flesh
       boats of their past as I walk toward
  what could be mountains or oceans, till finally
I am swimming through the lit window of a name.

Elegy (with Advertisement) Struggling to Find Its Hero

It was a century in which we touched ourselves in mirrors
over and over. It was a decade of fast yet permanent
memories. The kaleidoscope of pain

some inflicted on others seemed inexhaustible
as the positions of sex, a term
whose meaning is as hybridized as the latest orchid. Terrorism

had reached a new peak, and we gradually
didn't care which airline we got on, as long as the pilot
was sober, and the stash of pretzels, beer, and soft drinks

remained intact. On TV, a teenage idol has just crawled, dripping wet,
from the top of a giant Pepsi can, or maybe I imagined it,
flicking through channels where the panoply

of reality shows has begun to exorcise
the very notion of reality, for both the scrutinized actor
and the debilitated viewer who becomes confused and often reaches

into the pastel screen for his glass, while down Broadway
sirens provide a kind of glamorous chorus
for this script of history where everything is so neatly measured

in miles, pounds, or megabits. How nice it would be
to drowse in the immeasurable. How nice
it would be to escape.

And there's a wobbly marble bench
beneath an out-of-focus tree on the Web
I like to occasion my body with.

How brief we've become in our speed
I think. How fast the eternal.
How desperately

we need a clearing, a place
beyond, but not necessarily
of nature. *And the rain*

was so deep the entire forest smelled of stone, then the sun
broke, burying the long shadows
in gold. And the wounded

king woke in a book long since closed, and the princess
came to in a bed so large
she could never leave. How desperately

we need a new legend, one with a hero, tired
though he may be. One who has used
business to give up

business, one who has bought
with his heart what we
sold with ours.

The Irises

The irises were so beautiful I had trouble
leaving. One day, one day it will be lonely
when people go. I wanted to linger a bit
longer among irises. Some white, some purple,
some pale blue. What can one say among
irises? One's speech grows dumb as they touch
the air. I wanted to linger a bit longer
among irises. The moment moves. Are you
ready? I think the body's a mansion
with two doors, one luminescent and open,
one dark and closed. I wanted to linger
a bit longer among irises. I felt something
opening into the room among our tangled
arms. One day, one day it will be lonely. Petals,
paper doors, walls, clouds. I wanted to,
you wanted to. That your desire may spill
into eternity, an impatience whose lingering is all.

When I Died,

I saw a man tearing down a blue house
but inside the blue house a green house
slowly appeared as the man motioned
toward me, suggesting I enter, opening
a white door where the man became
a woman in a yellow field with snow falling
upon so many people walking toward
a blue house, and they were telling each other
they had never seen anything so green,
not even the grass under the red sky of their names.

Poem

Such a long way through darkness then a chance to sing.

Autumn seemed to mirror something as indiscernible as it was
green.

—Grass, straw, flame. The distance between each
is a sleep of seconds. What city would you
build?

And the air became rock, the earth
air, the fire
water, and the water a cloud we could feel
whose rain and spring sunlight

waited. And you could not breathe but were called. And you
waved and waved and waved
till the centuries of it
arrived.

Theory

A child's running hard toward the height of a man,
running, picking up shiny objects along the way,
and the man, having built a great tower, is gazing
down, squinting, trying to find the child. —To raise

memory to the vividness of the present. It was
a moment of hands, eyes, salt. Sheets, white, knew
flesh and let it sink. He remembers a blue shirt
slipping off a hanger. That was long ago, almost

a life. Now I'm learning to feel the invisible bones
of her face, dressing them with my own
dissolving touch. One theory of time's a moving knife's
edge, reflecting all, and all that it touches shines.

Yes

Sometimes in the middle of each April
when the dandelions stare
through our sleep, when the cellophane, torn,
glints in the teeth of grass, and the squirrel lobs its orange fire

limb to limb, I am content to gaze into the air engraved
with sparrows and rain, into the wonderfully out-of-focus
green in all its flux. Then the word *yes*
finds all its creeks and rivers, then our cries
are urgent and palpable as gravel thrown
into water. Surprised we
blink and are taken. Then I remember

that my question, having something to do with light, has come
a long way, and now I would like to tell you
something else in the language of petals, something about winter
and the stones placed upon so many dead.

Blueprint for Civilization
Sometimes Lost in Frivolous Detail

His archeological site's a junkyard where the lost sound of a car horn
becomes a city's screams of terror and joy.

* * *

The Abercrombie & Fitch ad shows the sweaty flanks and torsos
of boys moving toward a goal we could only guess
is youth multiplied by victory.

* * *

"And the Ancient of Days took his seat. His clothing was white as snow;
the hair of his head white like wool." Daniel 7 (9-10)

* * *

The cartoon showed Road Runner, having overshot the cliff's
edge, gazing down into pure consciousness, then the mad
scramble back to this earth.

* * *

She said to me, "To be close to God you have to go through a series of events.
You don't hear of many people speaking in tongues while they're
doing the dishes."

* * *

The traffic leads toward bleachers surrounding a spectacle.
And if you were to uncode the tall glass and concrete, what would
remain? —A forest leading up to a desert which becomes sea
where an immense orange light shines.

Psalm

And the tide came in and the tide went out. And when the sun set
over the burnt trees and toppled buildings, there was
a gilded loss.

And each of us had a little book, and we began
to gnaw on it till the words came
or we remained

dumb and silent. And each of us had a little stick
with which to walk, and we leaned
on them and looked over all

we had ruined. And each of us had a little bowl
and each began to pour its
contents into

another, and we did this over and over until all
the bowls had been poured and were
empty, then we

all smiled, holding nothing, and were happy.

The Field

I like the field best in winter when it's a giant bug

lying on its back, when its legs

are trees walking through sky. And I know

because they buried you in a field

the bug will right itself in a great spring

wind, dragging limbs through the earth, roots

through the clouds, and though you'll be

gone, I will have lost nothing

for that creature will carry the dead

like eggs to another earth

where they will swarm, and all our

remembering will be invisible tracings

in a familiar wind on a different sky.

American Urn

A wide prairie dotted with buffalo finding some mountains.

A machine on a long track moving west: People in feathered

costumes. —Flags, a slaughter. Below, a war with this flag

and another that, as you turn the bronze, becomes a modern

riot. Now a metropolis and airport, a radio tower,

then a dead tree that resembles a cross as the images become

more cluttered—an ad for soap that will make you younger,

a tiny action figure staring into the distance, and an enormous

shine from I can't tell what, but could be the evening

with all its bright tons settling down over wheated fields.

The Nest

In the room lit by one candle in a white building,
you could hear the whining of jets and the shivering
roar of trains. We sat in a circle as the man
handed out slips of paper and asked us
to write down the hardest thing in each of our lives.
Then he asked us all to return at the same time, one
week later. We did and sat in the same places
as he picked up the pieces of paper and began to read:
"forgiving my brother who raped me when I was
ten"; "saying goodbye to my mother as she slowly
died"; "watching the hate in my son's eyes as he left
and never returned." When he finished reading, all
the pieces of paper became birds, that room a dark forest.
We returned each week to hear them screeching, singing,
screeching, as the sun rose and kindled the bright leaves.

Gone

for Willis Barnstone

When we arrived from that world of 30,000 sleeps, some
who had forgotten asked how it was,

and moved by their pleas I replied. There
we wore suits of flesh, and with these
thought we loved, sometimes
pairing off for a life.

There, some of us prayed, others made art, but most
bought and sold things over and over
as if they were building

something. And every day there was either a lottery,
or a sacrifice, gleaming red on
a hill while others watched
in joy or fear.

There was a place with wide, palm-lined avenues
and casinos on either side where people
bet on wheels, cards, dice, which made them feel
alive and what they thought was happy.

I said that in spring, marveling at the green earth
and wet air, we made excited sounds with our red tongues and polished
    language
like so many twittering birds, except that we
were unable to lift our bodies.

I said that we were a small, blue green planet, a chrysalis
turning gray and brown, hung from a galaxy's
lit-arm, and that when you wake up

you would be here.

Long Portrait

The snow coming through that X-Ray is a mountain
no one can reach, but through a season's
melting becomes your bones.

Like it or not we belong to the dark.

Look, daffodils unfold beneath a jet's roar
while a red ball rolls across the lawn.

Remembering, I threw the spoon I fed you with into the ocean.

Love's the celebration, flesh the dangerous ice cream.

Twilight settles like the weightless talk of children.
—Stars, then a grave.

III.

Bright Hunger (2004)

"… animate
the trivial days and ram them with the sun…"
—W.B. Yeats, "Vacillation"

Once

—To whistle once into a forever wind.

And the light from the sky pooled around us.

We put our hands into it and rubbed it on others, ones distant
or gone.

And chance assigned us a time, and our bodies grew.

And we became aware, then our bodies grew tired, and our minds
were taken away.

Yes, some of us have been found, but what's lost often remains forever.

Sometimes in the middle of October an April occurs, and we marvel
at green bursting through the papery yellow,
then it snows and the sun comes out all across the white page.

And you stand there, dusted in a brightness, moving alone.

A Glass of Water

The stars, for the glimpsing,
for the gazing beyond. A crush of stars
heavy with the dark October sky.

Or red blood cells scattered on the slide's white
field. Worlds without, worlds within.

Yesterday, in the tall grass
by a creek below mountains and forming
mountains of cloud, there was
nothing I wanted to possess, I who love
the flesh so much and try to make
a house within poems.

When my clumsy hand first learned to write *yes*
I placed a sun over trees by a river
and realized much later
yes cannot be written. And *no* is a stone growing larger
until it shrinks, finally unnoticed
within a mountain.

Petru sang in the choir in Bucharest, sang in the choir
as a boy, and later worked as a barber in Auschwitz
where his jaw and teeth were broken.

Now he sells auto parts in Cleveland. He says
radiator and wipes the spit from his chin.
Marina, he says, *her name was Marina.*

Pour a glass of water in sunlight. Now lift
it toward your mouth and try to imagine
the same act in a fleshless world.

The sky's swarming with stars. To sing
nothing into being. Grass, trees,
and clouds. Just try.

Go

A small word with no end to it and a wind
that continues into another country.
A word that takes on a different meaning
after someone dies, a word that has a strange
engine that says, "Continue," but then continues
not to move as if burdened with its own
command, a breath which is all exhale. Once
in dream I was sent to the country of GO
with a message for the king who was dying
but seemed to understand, except that he was
unable to reply, then it turned out he
wasn't really a king after all, just a man,
and all the time I was hoping he would say
something like GO FORTH, which sounds kind of
cheery before you start to think about it. The
question now's not so much how to reconstruct
our lives, but how to stop the word that almost gets
to God before it's really gone. The word has
a hollow noise, an otherness beyond. So
what do we do? Does one simply
say, "Now, now," like firing blanks into eternity.

Passing

It is now   this late evening in April
among first irises and bees   I realize
they were opening doors   Mary   Robert
and William   I want to say of clouds   sunlight
rain now   Didn't we notice the arrows
of hearts   hands   leaping toward an unmapped
when   No age no place though all of one
light   Somewhere beneath that cloud
in a little town   a white door is opening
maybe for nothing but wind   but we will all
one day be there   I mean when opening is finally enough

An Autumn Essay

Everything happens at once, a world sifting its yellow
leaves to sing a lessening sun. The tulle wrapped around
the goldenrod and pupa
like a veil only found in cloudish

ways. On TV Sister Wendy spoke of Botticelli—
his name means little barrel. He stole
gold leaf to paint Venus' hair, and while Sister Wendy
spoke, Lisa's caterpillars hung from each of several

stems. Their larval bodies were beginning to change
as the first snow dusted the mountains—a fire
in us that said "go there." Someone we knew
was dying. He drove a silver Corvette for hundreds

of miles to watch the stars. His long white hair
blew in the wind while a monarch caterpillar
hung from a thread. Its green body
would swell and mummify to some pellucid

capsule, clearer and beyond, till one morning
we noticed the inlaid gold beads haloed
about the crown, and then—barely visible—
the apricot, yellow and black-striped

wings. Plato came to mind as I drove to see
my white-haired friend. We went fishing
at Monument Lake, and when the trout hit the elk
caddis, I knew it lessened the pain, just as the snow-capped

mountains and his mistress from Texas did.
She cooked fried green tomatoes with bacon with
trout. Another friend opened hundred dollar bottles
of wine. We smoked cigars and looked at the stars. No one

asked about the pain, but we remembered
the lake and fish. Everyone agreed it was the best
meal we'd ever had. We got drunk.
We danced. We turned the ranch upside down

and Joe forgot for awhile as we
walked long into the night and he talked of his family.
I remember he had a dog named Rocket,
dead now, but boys still call its name.

Water

                    Sunlight, brushstroke, sunlight. Worms
in a can, blood on a green sock, and the bluegill, crappie,
and perch all sunstruck.

                    —A fish gasping
in the seamless present, and some
gnats now, swirling before them, grainy now.

                    And the red cooler
and shiny cans of soda, and apples, all of these now
stuck like balloons, bunched, waving from the past,
reflections still shivering there, the boy
and father fishing beneath the dam.

Then the creaking of chains and gates opening,
and them running, dropping things— tackle box, poles,
stringer of fish as the huge white-bearded spray
pours down around them still slipping on a ledge
now, cutting their shins and hands, slipping through water,
now grabbing at rocks and limbs, adrenaline coursing their

bodies back to the car, where they collapse now
with the event still shedding its light like the scar
the sun burned through cloud into the larval
earth and into their brains, all of this, what they recall
half a century later, the heat and joy and wild panic to live.

Because

in that country we live only a day, how
slow the hours of each season. How we find
in each lingering now all moments
just as you once found in the cloud
of death one leaf of joy, and in that leaf
a rain of laughter within which lay
one hidden scream, unflowered. And while

in the spring of one morning a woman
watches tulips open and thinks of a man,
if you were to enlarge her invisible reach
you might see along the skin of her arms
thousands of tiny dice, and within

the black marks of each die, the turning
stars. And if you were to tape the birdsong
of that country, then play it back at an
infinitely slower speed, you would hear
within each silver chirp something like
the wheels of an enormous train rushing
toward an ocean you can't see but smell.

Rodeo

1.

        A child
we played with was whatever you wanted
him to be, but when we said, "tree," he
cried, so we became a forest and he cried
louder. So dark yet hopeful was

our wilderness. Still we like knowing
it's there. A place to go to get covered up
in, to forget, or to conceive ourselves, history
seeking animals. *Sixteen Candles,*

remember that song, marveling at our
youth again. The very trees
could sustain that wish, gently tossing
such precious green, back and forth. —Or

perhaps that we are still
so freshly arrived. —The girl,
fallen in the wheat, trying to reach
the weathered clapboard house that winded

occurs on the horizon. To colonize
means to continually sprawl
order out over the dark, and over the wild,
or as Sir George Peckham of "thys late

undertaken voyage" said, "as pleasing
to almightie God, as profitable to men.

For God did not mean for such souls
to languish amidst an uncleared
wilderness, creeping about in fearsome

2.

shadows." Back at the drive-in
gigantic dreamsize faces float across
a depthless stage. The summer
air is warm with sounds of Wiffle balls
and Hula-Hoops. A clean-shaven

father comes to a house where an aproned
mother waits, watches with held-breath.
And the dream is so big at times
the house seems empty. —Or maybe it's July
and evening, and kids are buying blue

Popsicles while sprinklers work the sultry
air to green the beautifully false
suburban lawns, as enchanting as
so many gushy whispering trees

to bored and greedy English-sailor eyes.
"For God did create lande, to the end
that it shold by Culture and Husbandrie,
yield things necessary for man's

life." What has that come to mean?
—from times when a slow wagon
got you there, to an electric
now when all the radio towers
loosen their voices and begin to lean

dangerously away from the past.
Someone must be listening, cheering
as the stadiums fill, the schools
empty, and the clock drags us out of

3.

nature. In a great midwestern city that had more rust
than people, I got down on my hands and knees
and prayed to the most constant thing
I knew, the soothing hum

of a generator. I witnessed a great peace transposed
to the landscape of bridges, rapid trains,
and terminals, remembering how as a kid,
looking up through a stripped

engine block, a slant gold light
strayed, gradually purpling down
each sleeve without piston. I gave each one
my hand, and dreamed
of a beauty timed

4.

beyond our bodies. Sweet Christ
it's so beautiful, the squared endless acres
ballooning a spun-gold light
as you head west on the Interstates
through Iowa, Nebraska, or Kansas.

An aluminum 16 wheeler, carrying the late sun
on its side, jack-knifes to avoid a car
and sails humpbacked like some fabulous
whale. The great wilderness

5.

snores. What felled desire! One summer
men walk clumsily on the moon, only
their breaths heavy as they touch
in slow motion

again and again that ash
body. The toy
flag, whose staff could not be
driven in, recalls

our own wild
impotence—wires to effect
the wind on a place
forbidden because made

6.

sacred. The KWIK-STOPS,
the GAS and GOs. How freely
we gad about. Once to know a place was to be
that place. We want so much
to explore, to glide down rivers of print
and down rivers of

film. Our new Don Giovanni's
the man who after 24 hours
sets himself on fire
in the adult video arcade? Does the poor
rodeo of our bodies

7.

progress anywhere unexpected? The Angus,
bludgeoned, gaffed, then hung up
to bleed, seemed an apotheosis
of the real. Men in white smocks

gradually took on
robes. Crushed steel led me to this further
carnival of flesh. Now in the church's
organ, I hear the *hummingwhine*

8.

of both. Will something please
happen. We're dreaming so very
hard, but there's a fever in the attic
of every house, a dog

barks furiously at our heels, and a sick
man's waiting for a heart.
I think I'll go
shopping. "The best heart

9.

money can buy." My wife
tells me I
have beautiful

10.

shirts. Wild we
were.

Before Us

When the bell rang we all seemed to wake up. Trees
yellowed, blood ran from our ears. First there
was too much screaming, then everyone was silent,
so we opened people's mouths looking for words.
They all looked the same, though occasionally
we found frozen cries, screams, shouts, still
reticently attacking the air like the leaves
of a red maple. With these we built
a glass city. The sun illumined its walls
and we waited the slow hours of eternity,
the winged filaments of light all our volatility.
So much we wanted to speak, but our
language seemed held in check by another
more painful language's architecture:
a language of loss and of love and of loss.
Seasons sped past. Winter gave green snow.
In spring the grass was red, and summers you
could watch the violet leaves speed toward
autumn's schizophrenia of color. The colors
spoke of forgiveness and our own wild profligate
lives. People said that if you spoke you
would die, but we were already living proof
of the dead, and at every moment you
could see through all of history.

My Father's Hats

Sunday mornings I would reach
high into his dark closet while standing
　　on a chair and tiptoeing reach
higher, touching, sometimes fumbling
　　the soft crowns and imagine
I was in a forest, wind hymning
　　through pines, where the musky scent
of rain clinging to damp earth was
　　his scent I loved, lingering on
bands, leather, and on the inner silk
　　crowns where I would smell his
hair and almost think I was being
　　held, or climbing a tree, touching
the yellow fruit, leaves whose scent
　　was that of clove in the godsome
air, as now, thinking of his fabulous
　　sleep, I stand on this canyon floor
and watch light slowly close
　　on water I'm not sure is there.

Potter's Field

And if death is poverty
we are rich now, having finally become

place now, shadowless we are
at peace. News only to earth

now, something to be
still for, over and over again.

So much easier to speak
now, as only wind

resembles our breath
now, as only waves

lap like tongues, our
only reach that of thirsty

green trees. Desire's
ravenous mouth gone

now. What we could not
save cannot be spent

now, though what we
loved remains, red

hearts parachuting,
for we are of earth now

and cannot fall again.

Poem

Rolling off our tongues and eyes, does the present
really exist?—as minutes swell into hours, days—
and that dream balloon, years later, rolls leadenly past.
Meanwhile your body's a long road on which I get lost.
I think of you often, but remember most when you
handed me that eraser and empty vase, a potential
emptiness I loved, for what we promise lies somewhat
mysteriously in the past. —Well, you know, as we're all
promised death in the slight wind of a word. When,
when, when, its breeze teases our faces toward a light
we can never quite have, as now, you hand me
this glass of water. Why does its glow seem longer
in evening? The future's a bore where those two
lovers are skeletons whose past was once cells dividing.
Therefore, let me pick thee some long-stemmed dandelions
where we will loiter and marry beneath that beautifully
bloated gold star we call the sun in evening.

Vermeer

It's the one where the woman
by a window is weighing pearls. She's holding
a balance, but it's empty, though there's gold—pearls
and stuff on the table. I must have been
twenty when I discovered it in a book on the third floor
of a student house. Everything was so loud: music and fucking
below. So I took the painting into a closet, pulled the metal
chain of the light switch and sat with the image
on the floor. She's pregnant and her head's tilted toward the light
all over her hands. I had a piece of paper and I needed
to write something, but the quiet wouldn't hold till I put
the foam earplugs in. Were those coins
on the table? And above her head some kind of painting
about heaven and hell. I could hear my blood
surge and the furious noise of my heart, then I began.

It's True

the dead have left us, but we have
not left them. They are tired of their toys—
stone, cloud, water. They want something
more—to touch a Popsicle melting, to feel
the heat on their faces, or to hold
for a moment the trout's shivering, reckless
glass, a present of the flesh
forgotten while the pillows of their prior sleep
move clouds, or centuries turn like pages
around their motionless hands. We'd like to speak
to them, but the graphs of our words
have long since become bridges of ash
dependent on winds to transport us
to some longing where—cloud-built and yearning
to be filled with a light. But we find them
again in the smell of cut grass, and in
things first seen—the burning stars, from which we,
fragile, hang featherweight tons of memory.

IV.

White City (2000)

"The way we had come was all we could see. . ."
—John Ashbery

White City

Shirtsleeved, walking out into the spring, occasionally
we glimpse a white city. We see it in the lilies
belled within shade, and its taste, like gin or lemon, slightly
burns the tongue. Mushrooms drop their spores, while a faint
static mixed with song strays from open windows. Winter's unremembrance
is gone. Flowers walk among our hands. We do not know
which touch is which. Sunlight drizzles through green, and the magnolia's
thick vanilla scent makes the mind go numb. This dislocation
which feeling is. Distant, fossil-boned, the city
shines. We approach it in our dreams, or see at dusk its thousand
yellow windows hived. Toward it invisibly we move
the way flowers move toward sun. Desire moves
in our wings.—Rain then sunlight shivers through cloud
until it seems the paper houses might dissolve. Irises poise
to unfold. Pollen blows across the ground, and in our houses
a bright-seamed light leaks beneath doors. We move
and are moved by what shines, and there is a distance
forever vanishing between our bodies.

X

Because every thought is either a memory or desire, the world

pulls away on both sides. Anyone's wish is a bird, and a wish

unfulfilled the unwinged skull, but a seed—fuzzy—pushes

its past toward tomorrow, all flutter and ecstasy. That's why

whenever I see people touch, I place a small white X where they

stood. Chalk, wind. Rock of sugar. Rock of salt. We spend our lives

licking at both. We sleep, eat, cry, sing. I like most when

it snows, when I must reinvent the shivering marvel of each

X, as knowledge is recollection, and love all discovery without delay.

No Continuing City

between two *whens* between
two *whens* man made a godflashthing

and the bees leaned deeply
into the flower. Please measure my weakness

with your power. What is
the half life of a moment? What beauty

is chance changing us
so quickly? More slowly, how sweetly

you blur the contours of my
body. The price of knowledge is

* * *

nature. And the quick jacket of light clothed everyone.
And the light was wedded
to the darkness. And the earth

was wedded to the sky. And the water
was wedded to the water. And the water
was wedded to the fire.

How dark into the far do the dead sail?

* * *

And the transom of light leapt to an ocean of shadow.

Pouring out over the bridges the knocking sound
of bodies.

            Pouring out over the bridges
the knocking sound of bodies.

                      —Words
in a verbflash torn out of their mouths.

* * *

And Jisenji Temple that had vanished
And the unopened tin of mandarin oranges
And the black rice and the black trees and the black people.

* * *

"Thou still unravish'd" now
let the act begin now let the bees
hungry gold priests drowse with the sweet taste

of —. What is that "lowing
at the skies?" Now "Lead'st thou
that heifer" and push the tungstening bright

flash down over the land?

Horse

On a metal table, a horse's heart and lungs.
I stare the slow miles down. July, the Rio

Grande's green tongue. Desert nights, crystal
animals, —a silver throw of stars. Constellations

stalked us: Love's incredible velocity
standing still. The left ventricle's giant balloon

still filled with blood: a rushing in my ears, wind
through juniper and sagebrush, on red rim

rock a clattering of hooves. *Will you, will you,*
I said. The coarse mane and straining neck,

the frantic whites of the eyes. The *Sangres*, snowy,
astonished us, as we were to each other, always close-

up & far away. The left ventricle courses fresh blood
throughout the horse's body. The right ventricle

sends blood to the ochreous lungs. Canyons sleep
in our straw hearts. Breathing is what saves

us. Anonymity lives in that rust-turreted land. We
made up new names, places without destination. I

once said *I love you*. Somewhere those words still
stand, a ruined adobe chimney. History changes easily

when people talk too much, or are simply struck
speechless. The skull's stark white light

frees us. Now I want to push my hands into each
of the heart's great cavities. My hands are heavy

& red with the earth. The horse is a great table
that holds and carries us over the land, selflessly.

Mansion of Happiness

People stand in front of a large white house giving
things away. June light floods the windows and occasionally
they look up as toward a familiar song. They stand on
the slow green hill of their lives. The air smells with rain
and the flowers are in want of their hands. They give
things away because their bodies are tired. Distant, a jet strays,
its tiny silver lozenge an impossible word. A woman says
"I remember Will" and a slight wind moves through the trees. Belief
is this language pulling them together, holding them
apart. The words need them so. Someone passes cookies
around on a silver tray. There are chairs everywhere
but no one is sitting down. How important it is to love
what is gone. Mary says "my son" and the word is handled
—clean and simple— like an egg peeled of its shell. Everywhere people
are whispering "I want you to have..." Detached from everything
they are open to all. Love's pollen flies. Dandelions spill
bright coins on the lawn. Shadows stretch out long. Trees pool
against sky, the pale joinery of clouds. A bird sings *how
long, how long*, while a boy listening to his Walkman, walks
down the road. Everyone turns and smiles. They watch him
watch the world. Soon they will go inside before the house is gone.

Discovery

Across the urban sky the slow bass sound
of jets, invisibly latticed, so many vibrating
strings. They are this century's music, a soft tearing
of air, a music of excoriation, a larger breathing

* * *

than us all. In gray November air, the museum's a dark canvas.
Outside, people pause and talk hesitantly
about real lives, too small or large

* * *

to be contained. Driving west in evening, in what seemed then
a larger dream, he stopped in a small mountain town.
Taking the map, the butcher traced
with sinewy fat and blood on his fingers
the fibrous sections of roads

* * *

through green. The grandmother dying, shrunken to half her weight,
looked out the sunny window of the nursing home
and said, "Look, there's our house." And the sad
thing was not the lack of recognition, as he held her bony
head up to the glass of water, and up to the aquarium's
larger glass walls, but that all of the houses looked

* * *

the same. Colorado, Wyoming, Utah. History
and freedom. The future of nature is dream.

* * *

The little girl's fingers all impatience
all over the silk bows of her presents. Mansion
of Happiness. April. The green hazel limb heavy
with the swarm's gluey gold. A kind
of fire in their bodies, inextinguishable because the queen
loves darkness. The words I heard after so much
breathing through cheap hotel walls in Kansas.
"You wouldn't have had to have had me,"

* * *

made me think that we are all divested travelers.—Space.
To what extent are astronauts dead men?
Or men trying fitfully to conceive? I kissed
Dorothy inside the Statue of Liberty. What a staid,
athletic pose. "Where are we going?"

she said. At the church everything was
conducted in the past. "Would you have taken
this man to be your..." "Yes, I would
have," she said. We left a little sad

* * *

but hopeful for that past. There is little as beautiful
as a bright yellow bulldozer
breaking into the dark earth
and moving it around, a big mechanical
sunflower shouting, grunting

* * *

some kind of love. The memory of being in someone's body
is not unlike remembering someone who has died.
What allows the physical to become bodiless

* * *

summons memory to replace desire. The suburbs
endlessly sprawl. They want to redeem us
but do not know how. I live
in a box with a window. There is a tree
I water on Sundays. No one ever

* * *

visits. When the hive swarms
the new piping queen is unlocked
to ensure the species.
All wing she loves

* * *

the darkness. The newspaper clipping said
he shot, but missed his sleeping wife.
"Just a bad dream," he confessed
to have said, soothing her back to sleep
before he shot and killed her

* * *

then later went to the movies. Imagine
having to imagine a wilderness,
unable to remember

* * *

one. Lewis and Clark reported a herd of buffalo
stretching farther than a man could

* * *

see. We live in a ravished world.
Once violence was real.

Even Now

Still I try to remember when you first caught
fire, the barely visible flames about shoulders and arms
accentuating every thing you touched, and I first saw
through words into their origins and hearts. I watched
you reach for a glass dissolving in air, while your
sight tore holes in an April world drowning
in rain and flowers. We walked through a park where
you stuck your hand in a young retriever's mouth, feeling
the hot pink gums and new teeth, while a little girl
wearing a ladybug cape swooped, singing over the grass
as bees droned *is, is* over the jonquils. We drove
to the country and walked through fields and meadows
and stood beneath an orchard's new gauze where you
talked of the past, picking chunks of time like invisible
fruit, and I could feel the rivers and trees engrave us.
We entered a half-built house, flooded with sky, and you
said, "There, there and there bodies will blossom."
I remember how it began to rain but you did not get
wet. How the fragrant wood smelled like a ripening fruit.
The sun came out as the evening grew long, and where
you lay down in the field to sleep there was only a red glow
resembling coals in a fire, a warmth I can feel, even now.

Anatomy

We touch the skeleton of a nameless man. We touch
his bones and hear their names: clavicle, scapula, sternum.
I touch vertebrae of the spine and see the tree a boy climbed.
I touch caged ribs. I would strum a song he loved, watch him
frame a house. Did he have a wife? I can see her scream
flower. There is wind. Wisps of cloud streak by.
I touch hands that will not hold seeds but whose phalanges
could rake the earth. I touch his feet and watch him brush
snow from the steps of a house. Look, there are guests arriving
to eat, talk, sleep. I touch smooth ears of the pelvis where
still the sacrum would flower, listening for stars. I touch the skull: orbits
where the eyes were, where light, ravenous, roving, lived. I touch
holes of the nose and mouth and watch a man wipe milk
from the lips of a girl he will kiss, trusting the marvelous flesh.
The class has one. Outside someone sings
and I feel everywhere the marvelous whiteness listening.

Serious Earth

A long metallic necklace of cars on an interchange
at dusk. —And then the noise starts again, and the crowd moves
toward the new stadium to watch what some think
games of darker-shadowed selves. O what they sing

and shout. In one tent a carefree, twelve-year-old girl
tries on her first bra, while in another a man twists
through the final elasticities of death. People grip their tickets,

moving from tent to tent. Look, there in the light
a great pile of spectacles. What men once looked through,
now only the sun finds, its final gold salve

a hymn too late. "Nevermind the past," one sings.
"The future is a beautiful deliberate machine: us
it aims." *If, if, if.* Was it immutable truth

or cartoon?—The pavilion marked *City of Boys*
sounded like so many engines, but is filled
only with trees, a nursery of spruce and pine. And then the noise
starts again as a man and woman begin to embrace

outside by the gate. See how the hands and fleshneck
give way to the marble face, and then the kiss is frozen
and suddenly they wake, surprised as strangers, and join
the shoving, pushing crowds down Joy and down Misery

Streets toward the main event. Inside a nodding man
reads, reads in a dim light—while others listen and wait—reads
from old telephone books, their paper cities stacked high, walled
up like impossible gates: Chicago, Denver, Albuquerque, Salt

Lake. He reads in the unspace between hands
the tiny black bridges of print. He reads what is
and what once was with equal grace: the giantism of lives
reduced to shuffling names and numbers. He goes on reading
and they go on listening too late, waiting to be called, waiting not to sleep.

These Cars

are the tired words around a city's great
walls. Mystery is speed. Listen, get

in. Beneath the dashboard's lamp
the map begins to resemble an animal's
insides. We breathe. The freeway

expands. Bodies of jets pass
low overhead, 1/2 spaceship 1/2
god. Civilization has stenciled our lives
so we might avoid that chaos

we crave. Nights with stars. You could hear
the cities dripping upward
toward their centers. That was before

the word had become motor. *Hurry
up, I can't hear you. Drive
faster.* The future

unspools and the dead grow closer
with each page of concrete
poured. But what

we are here for
must somehow be spoken
beyond where the bridges make
a thwanging sense

of the land. *Shhh*. I'm whispering
faster, farther, disappearing
into less. I'm

saying I love you I'm
wrapping the word around
your body.

Autumnal

The saffron-colored leaves are cresting into their moment. It's
the impinging lateness of things that's scary. Rusting,
rushing leaves now astonish, omitting what
they began to say. I saw people standing
in a circle on a hill, and the youthfulness of bodies
slowly began to separate toward soul. Perhaps forgetfulness
is a way of cleansing the far. I saw a woman
with yellow hands and red lips weave
through the circle. She spoke but one word and they
loved her. Their names were leaves in no
hurry. Her lips were the world's cherry. They said,
"Stop," then "Go faster," while the grapes' purpling scent
pierced the air and each brick of the old house
seemed an impossible slowly melting hour. I saw
the kite in the air. "The wind must be greater than the weight
of the string and its body."—Clouds, sun illumined
their marrow. The slow furiousness of leaves
blew at our feet. "Give it some string," he said, "and feel
how strong the pull." The man carried the kite
home. The leaves are nothing but words. How wonderful
it is to be here. And because we are not gone, still we are early.

Buffalo

They are the earth we have forgotten.
And the great continent of the head knows this
and will look right through you from the brown stones
of the eyes. And I would know them as a child knows
the brown-humped land that listens
for the prairie wind that is the bellows of their lungs.
A friend and I once stopped, astonished by the mile-long
herd, and by the slow train of the hooves
drumming up an expiring music like wind like God like sun.
Still I marvel as the late Nebraska light gilds the horns
and the ponderous mass of fur, while the foothills blue,
recalling the cold declining length of the rifle's bore.
They are the color of the earth thrust up, and history
still roams in the matted rags of hair, in the bleached litter
of bones, and in the chalky cliffs of the skull.

The Sheer Weight of History

lessens, as after years the weight of actions
lessens, becomes light as feathers, though their lessons
still the mind. The torturer's weapons recede into his name,
his name into the war's, its shadow lessened
by distance and by other shadows drizzling over

other names. It's almost as if we didn't listen
when the present fleshed the years with lives, when love
seemed possible and often was that eternity we
became bored with, and so acted out the *yes*
or *no*, or merely waited for someone else's

action. Now like innocence it's something past
losing: balloons rising, just out of reach
from the child's struggling hand that gradually becomes
a kind of helpless, happy wave? And so we look up

and back where history is a fat old man
who by telling stories to children gradually lightens
till all his weight is theirs, and suddenly
they are older. Was it thought that gradually

handed us over to becoming? As though some
child, ghosting up the rainy windows, drew figures till
the daydream blurred to action, and those actions
froze, drifting farther behind

his bearded hand. The stone chimney
still remains amid the vacant field, while discoveries,
declarations span the air like invisible bridges
or the fading contrails of jets we know

are there. Are they? We are the flame, history
the fabulous shadow where forms
no longer crumble, an eternity
made to measure what the shivering imperfect flesh

did. Names, deeds, numbers. More and more
we feel them lessen as we grow older, listening
more intently as the new snow falls, singing *once,*
always, lifting something up, covering the dark with feathers.

Sparrow

There is something I must tell you. Slowly we are vanishing
as I speak.—Something like hunger, faintly

beginning to stir from far off. Something
out of darkness, bulb or root pushing against the rain's

tongue. *Shhh,* the half-deaf boy said. *GGGod*
is a sparrow. The mangled words fell out

as he pushed his nose against the spirea's white
blossom goldloud with bees. Among so many

wings, language seemed
a ruined kite. Push his bike in,

out of the rain? Or leave it there later
for the dripping sun? Spring whispers things to you

out of sync. Fleck of this, fleck of that. Cardinal, or tulip
path.—Lips! What? What you didn't

say to her in jamcellar, then barn. Light splintered
and shot through the slats. Her taste, salt

in the rain. Page after page of it. Now sing
the way the straw makes its little shout against green

till the fire eats it and the real joy begins to shine like the sun.

V.

Quick, Now, Always (1996)

"For even the nearest moment is far from mankind."
—Rilke, Seventh Duino Elegy

Vista

for Ron Kroutel

I can almost recognize this from the hill,
the grey ribbon of highway leading into town, the overpass, its
antique colonnade shouldering the sun, and the way the sky falls
like blue snow through the steel towers
of the Electrical Park

locking everything into place. Home
looks out a picture window
that looks out upon trees
where a few deer stray like words
on a screen. We are so lonely

for this view, lonely to make
words in the small world
inside our homes. And while the children
were singing the squat snowman up, Sal
was dying in his garage. Sal who built

most of these homes. And then Willa screaming
off the deck, "Sal is dead." The words
hang there still, somewhere between
the gas barbecue and pool. And then we all wrote
cards: "Willa, deepest regards for you

in this difficult time." —Words
shy, words that kept slipping off
the page. It's summer now, that's why I say
I can almost recognize all this from the hill. I can still see

Sal. He dug the foundation for most of our
homes. He was the yellow hat and tiny waving hand
sitting high up in the backhoe's brain. I watched him
push rocky chunks of ground. Once his dirt-caked hands
lifted me high with the words "Did you

know I built your Dad's home?" I remember
that, and I remember Willa's scream: blue
electric words that still hang in the air
between the gas barbecue and pool. That was the day
the mailman disappeared into the woods.

Buffalo Nickel

Listen, can you hear the faint drone of sirens
moving through a river of cars? They are a violence
tattooed on cities, and we lean like plants
from the stems of our bodies, lean as toward

* * *

the drone of the sea. We need a new coin
with a jet on one side and on the other,
God. What would he look like?—Jambalaya
of noise.—A city's recrudescence

* * *

of glare. *Engine Rock*, aboriginal its orangish-
red glow.—Reptilian, all escarpment and scale.
Ochre are its bones, bleached pink and lavender its ashy

* * *

halo. The Nebraskan sun gold on their horns,
at dusk their wooly hair like smoke. As a boy in New York
I touched one, held the clear, bright language of myth

* * *

on a nickel. Wilderness is where
we never wander. And where, and where

* * *

and where. Dusk, the ghostly pastels of a few TVs
shimmer in Taos Pueblo. Where the creek divides
the kivas, a few beer cans tinsel the ground.—Trash

* * *

offerings up to some divinity? What did you
discover today? In La Junta, a man was trampled
by his own horses. The limits of the land,

* * *

the limits of the body. Buffalo, brown-matted fungus of God.
Home is not here, but there, not now, but then.

The Juvescence of Autumn

At dusk the ambulance came
pulling all the way up onto the lawn
like a red speedboat drifting

* * *

ashore. She was old.
She had fallen and broken her pelvis
while picking apples. She had

* * *

pruned that tree so many times
it appeared as a dark
hood. About it her white

* * *

head moved. The attendants, unloading
the gurney, argued about whose turn
it was to buy the pizza. I had been

* * *

sitting outside, reading beneath the yellow
leaves. I heard the thin
cry. She said to call, but that she

* * *

was OK, except for the pain. Then there was
nothing to say. We stared at the apples
still nested in their thick green hive. She talked

* * *

of a daughter, her grandchildren, her
dead husband, Karl. Still she stared
at the tree, talking as if the fruit

* * *

restored memory. That was the day a *streaker*
ran all the way down Bellflower Lane.
The sudden white breasts, — the pale shadow

* * *

between legs. Now I finally remember
what I wanted to say. —The silver thread
of the siren the ambulance followed

* * *

away. And that tree, the swollen
green crown, on which the apples were cities
opening far out onto an invisible world.

Tomato Soup

The simplicity of unadorned taste:
tomatoes, flour, salt. Unceremonious
and so unlike an English stew.

No hidden bones, chunks of meat.
No skeletons in our closet.
Can of soup, can of water.

You eat it after doing simple things:
skating, skiing, or just taking a walk
down a street of look-alike homes.

No iron kettle to hide ingredients.
A stainless steel pot on an electric range
works best. Do not add salt or pepper.

The simplicity of unadorned taste.
We love it the way the Italians
love tomato sauce with basil:

as a stronghold of culture,
a stubborn remembrance of revolution,
of green vines tied to stakes
and the pendulous warm red fruit.

Domestic

for Heather Utrata

December, and it would be a Saturday, some milk
out for the cat, as the long grey evening expires with snow.
He would read and she would color,
her face pressed right up
against the window of the paper. What does
she see?—Her heart one joy as the crayon-thick sun
pours yellow out onto the green trees
and large white box, beneath whose triangular hat
they will argue, love, dream, fight, and grow
up in. *House.* The very word's
a breathing out of so much
breathing in,—a book, a brain,
a wild brilliance of light trying to comprehend the dark air.

White

My father is dead, yet
how beautiful the snow.
For weeks now I've
done nothing, no thing

at all. But today
I stare out my window
and watch the snow
fall. Heavily, more heavily

still, the thick white flakes
soon mask the air, and slowly
I begin the long walk through
fields. There a white church

stands, but I do not
go in, no, I just stare
slowly stare until slowly
that church disappears.

Orpheus

Before the end, before the lovers spoke only in numbers,
before the photographs replaced memory, before vanity became a form
of passion and chic men and women stood idly before the great
airports of death, Orpheus

departed, the sheer ambulance of his calm
appalling. And as he guided her toward that light
he sang her whole again, marveling as if for the first time
at hair, ankles, hips, thighs, till the poem
became body, till the lilting rhythm

became her breath, the enjambed lines her reaching
arms, the lyric song an echo
saying, "Look at me, look at the pleasurewash
of creation. Feel the marble now
fleshwarm with salt.—Take

me." He turned once forever. He turned once for every
living thing, and the green waves of the dead became trees
lifted from their graves, listening. He turned,
beating the immense immeasurable wings of his song
against the sky of what he knew, of what he knew he had created

from death, of what he had learned from stones, touchdumb
but like her still shivering. He turned
once and turned back willing to be dismembered
so that the fragmented and mounting song
could rise a thousand times more beautiful against nothing.

Warhol

for Peter Schjeldahl

I watched the working class work and it bored me
to beauty. Something I found in light bulbs,
sometimes in shoes. Think of it,

a little light shining on someone's empty
shoes, such a small opera, and so ordinary,
but it was the car wrecks

that really saved me. Not that beauty was the beginning
of something scary, but that the scary was beginning
to seem really pretty. Violence

is just so handy, and sometimes love gets
bored to terror. Anyway, so I take
a chair, smear it with lavender,

but it's an electric one. The chair, I mean,
then something begins to happen, a pasteled
violence we can live with, a lavender

disaster. Then the *Maos* and *Marilyns* become
kind of car wrecks, too, but ones
with civilization and culture. Bigger, too!

Portraits so splashy and sugary you could eat them.
Rapture behind which a country's steely
menace grins. I mean

at best we are always watching ourselves
watch. Largely-happy-people
smile, pasted up on so many walls.

I am the world's voyeur, so wallflower
and wooden as to make things sizzle. I love
by remaining indifferent. This is my business, my leisure.

Woolworth's

for Gerald Stern

Everything stands wondrously multicolored
and at attention in the always Christmas air.
What scent lingers unrecognizably
between that of popcorn, grilled cheese sandwiches,

malted milkballs, and parakeets? Maybe you came here
in winter to buy your daughter a hamster
and were detained by the bin

of *Multicolored Thongs*, four pair
for a dollar. Maybe you came here to buy
some envelopes, the light blue *par avion* ones

with airplanes, but caught yourself, lost,
daydreaming, saying *it's too late* over the glassy
diorama of cakes and pies. Maybe you came here

to buy a lampshade, the fake crimped
kind, and suddenly you remember
your grandmother, dead

twenty years, floating through the old
house like a curtain. Maybe you're retired,
on Social Security, and came here for the *Roast*

Turkey Dinner, or the *Liver and Onions*,
or just to stare into a black circle
of coffee and to get warm. Or maybe

the big church down the street is closed
now during the day, and you're homeless and poor,
or you're rich, or it doesn't matter what you are

with a little loose change jangling in your pocket,
begging to be spent, because you wandered in
and somewhere between the bin of animal crackers

and the little zoo in the back of the store
you lost something, and because you came here
not to forget, but to remember to live.

Grand Canyon

Red rock
Sheered by the sun's
Drizzling rays; a steeped haze drops, descends
3/4's of a mile
Into the smoky blue
Shade. Down

We move
Through a thousand runneled buttes,
Eroded Byzantiums
Of red-ignited
Sandstone and shale. Pinnacles and minarets
Flame; towers, arches, domes
Dissolve into shadowy plateaus. To the east,

Bruise-blue,
Vishnu's Temple and Wotan's Throne
Support the sky. Above, the putty-white colonnades
—Osiris, Isis— shine.

The canyon walls balloon
With light. Clouds,

Cumulus, drag
Brief lakes of shade.
Purples avalanche grey
Into the inner
Gorge. Down,

Leveling out now
Onto the Tonto Plain,
Its dead sea floor a grey
Reptile head. Cremation
Creek's a pulp of
Dust; heat

Floods up. No
Sound. The last
Sunclad rocks, a skink
Freezes on stone. The sky

Indigo drowsed gold, a jet's
Contrail, the first
Narcotic stars. A cocooned stillness
Tugs us on. Listening
Like children in the storydusk,
We descend toward the river's
Green tongue.

History's Pause

The way maps gradually evolve
toward a kind of truth: Those few cumulus clouds
on a hot Sangre de Cristo afternoon
boiling together to form small continents of

* * *

rain. Rivers divide. Somewhere a child
pulls the threads from an orange. Yellow frontiers
become green territories become organized

* * *

states. In the pupal stage
the larva completely
dissolves. Have you noticed how
in cities the horizon

* * *

disappears? The will of one man
to build a ranch.—From continent's edge,
to horse corral, to his son's
crib. What we cannot enclose

* * *

will not die. New Mexico,
an inextinguishable yellow light
rises up out of

* * *

the land. *Taos, Truth or Consequences, Alamogordo, White Sands.* Cowboys &

* * *

Indians. Explosion, Sunset.
　　Explosion,

* * *

Sunset. Jefferson said: My father was a warrior
so that his son could become a farmer
so that his son could become a

* * *

poet. Hope lay west. From some stationary,
or dead observer, events would appear
to speed up toward

* * *

the horizon. The Golden
Arches of *McDonalds. Shell*
gasoline. Yellow

* * *

without. Yellow
within. One million videos
and films, small rivers within culture
leading to an unknown

* * *

where. The contemporary mind
resembles a transistor radio
at night. The roving dial,
the signal that will

* * *

not hold. The cool pastels of a TV
splash across the walls
of the world's

* * *

cartoon. A child rubs his hand
over this late at night. Free we ran

* * *

over the wide open
earth. And love, poor love
atlased beyond our hearts.

The Face

Wild and naïve,

        always just beyond because of the eyes
        their mystery water rivering out

        time. On the slow field of a cheek
        I have watched blond windlight bend

In a pasturing
curve, the smile's gradual
flood saying come quickly, come quickly

        lest the entire ocean of its
        salt you

Crave change, always, naked and already with-
drawing what you can-
not have.

Robert Mapplethorpe's Photograph of Apollo (1988)

What's missing is the body, its nakedness wrapped
in marble. What's missing is the hair, the floating hair
that falls in chalky tendrils. Only the face, huge
and larval-white, peers into the darkness.
Still, this is perfect youthful manhood, iridescent
against chaos. The eyes, wild and vacant, look
but see nothing. What slaking difference?—
They have known ecstasy, that patina
marble carries everywhere. A suddenness
unwarranted, beautiful. The lips, moistened, part
more to breathe than speak. Such desire,
a poetry. The silk of the moment before him,
the rest becomes salt, memory, history.
There is order here, but passion is its spectacular
disarray. The music turning toward light
shadows. O god of the healing art
where is the beautiful lyre of the body?

Heart

It snowed, a white beyond our knowing, and then
it snowed some more. The people, they were astounded,
as if some thing were born

of nothing, for that whiteness made an everything
from nothing, a nothing we could not name
but to which we prayed, prayed without knowing,

which seemed the only way, now
that our century darkened, darkened to a close,
and we were less, less than something whole,

for we had murdered something we could
not name, and that something fell, fell
more beautifully in its blankness

and in its cold, a cold that blew beyond
our knowing, and beyond our hearts' desire to know.

VI.

Against the Meanwhile (3 Elegies)

(1988)

I. The Wisdom of the Body

"Once, everything only once. Once and no more. And we too, once. Never again. But to have been this once…"

—Rilke, The Duino Elegies

1

April. The day is all middle.
The listening soil in light of all else.
I carry the trout to the garden,
lay them on the wooden table.

An hour ago
their gills were hearts of color
flashing like tulips from the water.
Now their mouths open and close on no

water, this slower knife.

My thumbs pray on the spilt middle,
scraping away the floral waste
as the body quakes in a final arch—
everything inside going out.

These still bright organs
belong in the earth to grow dull
quick under the tickling legs of flies and ants—
their telling stench
like the female scent to the male.

2

How the body goes on talking.
You make pots and vases.
You tuck and knead the clay.
Your lovely hands rub the woman into the work
you glaze and fire.

Behind your studio is another kiln, larger,
faster to end with less,
the fetid odor of burning flesh:
corpses of the poor.

The attendants do little.
Polishing their cars, they wait for bodies.
How much can one grow accustomed to?

The body dressed in flames will slightly rise
as if to sit.

3

Light is what lacks in each of us.
The body is drawn toward light.

Hundreds of ants
line the walk to the garden.
They steer in perfect files,
an unswerving syntax between tiny monuments.
The sun is their compass.

If placed in an open tube
with food at one end,
the larva of the brown tail moth
will crawl toward the light
and die of starvation.
The halo of desire.

4

I weed and turn the garden.
Everywhere there are worms
sliding through the rings of themselves.
All touch, they love the dark.

I hoe the soil fine as sand
then plant mustard seeds.
Small things become each other,
each grain with the hill of the ant.
Their houses are little clocks

and they too have gardens,
underground chambers
where bits of fruit mixed with excrement
form tiny acres of bacteria.
They feed off cultures that go on and on.

Spinach, peas, lettuce —
Then last, tomatoes and pumpkins.
In dusk-light the soil looks blue,
then goes slate

                      deep as water
as the stars appear.

5

Summer morning, the day before the solstice.
The trees are gauzed with light.
It is the time of domes and steeples,
and blond-headed children running home late.

I remember six months back:
the small day at five o'clock
like a piece of coal on fire,
a halo of tangerine on black.
The year seen through a camera;
this the final image of that.

Lettuce and spinach unfold in the mist.
The garden's a tent of oxygen,
the earth a world of insects.

The lacewing's body is the color of lettuce.
Green, faint as the beginning of any seedling.
Almost transparent.
I can almost see through the body.

6

Termites have taken over the stump.
Near the base, beneath the rotted bark,
a kingdom of larvae.
Snow-white eggs in the silken dirt.

How the large one, having lost a wing,
drags itself away —
perhaps to shed the other?

Is she a queen?
For the nuptial pair have wings
they lose after mating,
as if to say —
Flight is required,
conception an airy thing.

For the bird and insect,
wings are organs.
Flight a conceiving of space.
The bird a perfect center.

7

The languor of this longest of evenings.
What used to be called *Mid-Summer Night's Eve.*
How mistletoe was held to be sacred
seen in the sun's fire
at the two turning points of the year.
If picked at midnight
and thrown into the air,
the place where it landed would reveal the earth
in a blue flame.

In December
when the oak is bare,
its green leaves are an April,
its berries white as tubers.

There are times when the world reveals itself.
We look through our lives,
or perhaps the earth is looking through us.

8

Tonight as you
draw your knees to your chest,
I remember another inseparable space,
feel its close pulse

as now your body curves
to question,
and then by questioning
answer mine.

The wisdom of the body.

And so you sleep and I get up
and walk to the porch
where all night a moth taps the bulb.

Mistletoe, I think,
and how two doves led Aeneas
through a woods to find it.
The trick he used to catch the ferryman
and ride the river Styx to hell.
How deep that bark
sank with his living weight.

9

Today is October.
Except for the pumpkins everything's spent —
the last fruits of the sun's fire.
On one dead, already dry vine,
a cocoon's swollen pustule.
I separate the dry pod from the stem,
then split it with my thumb to find
a thick and formless jell —

the caterpillar gone,
dissolved to a fetal pool of white.
Its center diminished to everywhere.

We too once moved in a sleep like nothing
when liquids giving form
spelled out time's possibility.
So too when put in the earth
the body gives up shape.

10

The afternoon's a theater of orange,
each dry sound
a shade of darker growing color:
the ochre snap of weeds, the faint tock of dropping leaves.

Three o'clock in the afternoon
when for a moment the day pauses
with the weight of itself.

A school bus groans and brakes to a stop.
The children are returning to their imaginary worlds.
I hear their laughter through the window,
I feel its color through the glass.

Bees doze on the sill,
feeding on the warmth of the house.
They are their own last flower.
Their target bodies never miss.

11

Evening and everything is falling.
The sun is the weighted end of a wheel
and the trees are gears crumbling away in color.
No longer a movement

they stand like wooden fixtures,
monuments to space unfolding
as the stars begin to appear

and you stare at the paling sky
and weigh nothing.

II. Against the Meanwhile

*"So then I found in all things good
and evil, love and wrath, in creatures
of reason as well as in wood, in stone,
in earth, in the elements, in men and
animals. Withal, I considered the little
spark 'man' and what it might be
esteemed to be by God in comparison
with this great work of heaven and
earth.*

*"In consequence I grew very melan-
choly, and what is written, though I
knew it well, could not console me."*

—Jakob Boehme

Point Nine

1

Memory—hardly through the dusk
do the letters of that word break.
A boy calls his brother.
What the other boy walking home thinks
tossing the white ball up from the mitt —

                           then catching it,

the wandering present of the day's events
that in twenty years
will stray through the past
the way twilight strays toward the end of a street
then simply disappears
like the aggregate of shadow through leaves,
or the color of space beneath his bed.

    I will never forget
the first time I touched a leaf
etched in stone. The faint stir
like a wing through my spine. I
pressed it hard against my cheek
and hoped the mark would stay.
In half an hour it had vanished.

      Now, even the sand imprint
      blurs on that fossil.

Like history, we grow tired of things.
And they grow tired of us.

Near Pompeii, at the foot of Mount Vesuvius,
lies Herculaneum, the small village, now museum,
once buried in lava. A man and wife were found
embraced, caught in the soft stone.

As though love were the fossil of desire.

2

I stare at the zero ocean,
think of its vast decimaled floor.
How sun eases through the surface
diffusing light with darkness
in this mildly shuttered room
where indistinguishable bands of blue
fade to violet.

          And as you descend further
what you believe to be lack of color,
what you believe to be black
is only the depth

         the perfection of violet
until within the eye
only the vague tint lingers
within the breathing gills of the iris.

And whether you travel up,
or whether you travel down into water
                              you will learn
about space through the same shades of color —
blue both circle and center.

Point Eight

1

Cybele, I begin with you
who rose from the black stone
where nothing grows
and so became mother to all
in the endless cycle
of animal, mineral, and vegetal.

I do not know much about science,
but I know that nature
miniaturizes the world to possess it,
and that evolution is all.

Not the evolution of man,
bird, fish, insect, or plant —
but of the infinitely small
which moves toward something much larger
like the conflagration of a star
and the loss of mass

that streams toward us
when hydrogen nuclei
combine to form helium.

What we gain is called sunlight.

2

Now I know why Dionysus
held council at night, why he
crowned women's heads with flowers
and poured wine into their silver cups
                              till morning
when Apollo,
with gold-filleted locks
streaming onto his shoulders, stood
envious, that from such chaos
came order.

3

Entropy is such a god,
what it has become for us.

At Oak Ridge, Tennessee,
neutrons are slowed
in a swimming-pool reactor,
their trace, a visible blue glow
like the blush of science
upon man.

4

When the egg weds with the sperm,
the fertilized cell
cleaves once, twice longwise
then finally across
to separate the animal part
from the yolk it feeds upon.

The upper living part
feeding from below
goes on and on dividing
a thousand times
with no increase in size

until the blastula appears,
its hollow sphere with a thin roof
a smaller model of the world.

I think this inward movement
in which life begins
must be like that moment

                          when a child
looks at trees from a distance
and the blue evening bends all about
to cup their greenness.

Point Five

Heraclitus, who talked
of fire and sleep, said it.
The only reality

is change. What habit repels
to make life easy: our false
dream of continuity, the tropics of leisure

whose warmth dulls our sense of time.
Sunday morning after the party,
the little scuffs on the wooden floor,

record of joy and dancing
that in an hour will be waxed away.
Forgetting's gloss of memory.

2

Desire, too, is change.
I imagine a great fire
consuming abandoned tenements.
The hot wind blowing out windows
while among the bystanders who eagerly watch,

the arsonist himself
stands relieved
as flaming beams
collapse, wood
to ash.

3

Fear, too, is change,
where the borders of desire
close, and all roads turn back
to the capital
of need.

Or hope. What at times
we abandon,
and accept for a moment
the present, whose promise lies
in that it offers none.

Point Four

1

We are merely
a planet, speck of
that ongoing explosion
in which everything moves
outwardly. Galaxies equally receding,

centuries to them,
fireworks. Our lives, the held moment
when a roman candle
blossoms. Pompeii

to Hiroshima mere seconds, ephemera
of frozen color. Or on
a warm spring day
the viburnums' rush of pollen.

2

Like a dream fork
the tree of all species slowly
dividing, the one-celled protozoa
developing into slime mold
from which the first flat worm crawled?

3

Sometimes before sleep
or at some midpoint in the afternoon
when the sunlight falls watery through leaves,
my sight blurs into green
and I feel the presence of a body

all shoulders
struggling to hold
to the present
down whose steep bank it goes
slipping back forever.

4

Millions of years ago
when the rivers of South America dried
and fish lay strewn on the banks
groping for water, only
the mutants,
those with small gills
survived, burying themselves in silt,
breathing slowly
until the rains, the water might rise.

5

In the continual dawn by the sea
two men play chess.
The stakes are death. The game
hinges on a chain of mistakes
the winner will have made
all in his mind.
They sit in a rapturous
poise. The only consciousness
is change, and evolution is
a perpetuation of errors.

6

The world goes on getting richer,
even in poverty
the detritus piles up:
bottles, cans, and worn-out
tires, the movement only partially stopped.

Perhaps salvation means
to die
just as one's goods entirely run out.
Bartleby faces the wall,
his last words

    "I would prefer not to"

a wish to complete
his only remaining task
denied. The piety of such loss
like touching the face of God
or counting the bricks in that wall.

7

Or why the accused
takes the executioner's knife
and twists it
into his own chest. A final leap
of humility
to simplify the task.

The saintly life of deprivation
whose common denominator is loss.

An old woman sits
staring into the future.
The uncashed check in her hand,
her son
dead. This is a wind like time.

Point Three

1

This junkyard stretches for miles,
a cemetery of wrecked cars
some of which passed through red lights,
others hurtled off roads.

Hoods and fenders collapsed,
window glass shattered in accidents,
the perfect coincidence of time and space.

Hot rods groomed for high performance
and luxury sedans once handsomely chauffeured
now all move at a standstill, ruled by
only the sun. Paint blisters,
thousands of hubcaps wink
and headlights doze in vacant stares.

Pokeweed and sumac grow wild
among the matted grass and jacked-up cars.
And like ants on something sweet,
men crawl about here looking for parts.

2

Over there an old Impala,
its left rear door swung open,
leans beside a tree.
A leg of ivy elegantly crawls
upon the mildewed carpet,
velour, and rotted foam of seats.

Nearby, two abandoned truck springs
spiral with trumpet and honeysuckle vine.
Cream and yellow blossoms
fountain among the junk,
while everywhere like common currency
wheel wells rust

into ochre and ferrous shades.
Miniature western landscapes,
perfect circles of sunlit flame.

I stare at a stripped-down engine block.
Each of the pistons, once
so perfectly timed, now
forever stopped.

Little teeth of rust like gears
continue to take them apart
as the long exchange begins,
machinery's slow grind
back into the earth.

3

I walk on and on through miles of debris
and look out over a hill, a horizon
filled with windshields.
To understand America, visit
a junkyard in spring.

Stepping over drive shafts,
strewn among wild parsnip and yarrow
where the bees like tiny gold phantoms
persist and continue to work,

I begin to see
how each of our minds resembles
a junkyard of the past.
All that we wish had happened
cheated by time or place.

Before me, an old Chevy lies
surrounded by tall, cabbage-laced blossoms.
I rub my hand along its side,
sprinkle rust among the pollen,

knowing that tonight
as I lie at home in bed,
here the axle of stars will continue to turn,
turn above this place.

Point Two

1

I sit on the sand by the ocean,
adding sticks to the fire
as the rain, infinitely gentle, begins
dousing away the flames,
petals growing back
into the flower's charred center.

Now I think about history
compared with the smaller endurance
of air, fire, water, earth;

the way time sanctifies memory
yet in desire both collapse.

If unable to remember
would there be any sense of time?
Or would we all move about like ants
who only momentarily pause
touching muzzles over their dead?

I think of the great explorers,
that still moment of discovery
reconciled with time.

Magellan gazing out over the Pacific,
forgetting what for.

VII.

The Halo of Desire (1987)

". . . Perhaps the blue color of water
and ice is due to the light and air they
contain, and the most transparent is
the bluest. Ice is an interesting subject
for contemplation . . . Why is it that a
bucket of water soon becomes putrid,
but frozen remains sweet forever? It
is commonly said that this is the
difference between the affections and
the intellect."

—Thoreau

The Distance of Flesh

is a sadness, yet still
I place this picture of you
in a scrapbook,
thumbing by chance to a photograph
of your father's just-wed parents.

Their faces shine like coins,
yet live only in memory
as does your father
whose death
left your mother half alive.

As kids we threw pennies in a pond
to see some kissing goldfish.
Their mouths seemed locked for hours.
So close, we could have dreamed them.
As close as loss itself.

Once I saw a man
set himself on fire.
His body lit in flames kept lifting up
as if to stand and walk away,
the tired hero of a film.

I say I'll forget
but I can't.
To forgo the love of flesh
one must be a saint.

I toss this scrapbook in the fire.
I can't look at photos.
The distance of flesh is a sadness,
the body's soul a doll on earth
passed from heir to heir.

Dandelions

To see their heads
by low sun,
spheres that seem to rise
like tiny balloons, illumined
and buoyed with light,
is to understand their vacancy.

Watching them closely —
trying to decide
what color grows there,
frail as the curls
of cigarette smoke
around an old man's face,
or blurred
like the circular flick
of bicycle spokes
when a child pedals away.

As a boy, getting
on my hands and knees,
looking through the eye of one,
a camera's lens
out of focus.
The colors were the same —
like seeing glass through glass.

Now by moonlight,
moons themselves —
less bold though,
shy as a film's negative
waiting to be developed.

They cast no shadow.
Heads hold a faint glow
still allowing transparency.
One looks through seeds
at the thimble
from which they grow—
that which dies.

My thoughts rise
in the dark now
like the faint balloons
these dandelions once were.
They each carry
a small dream into night.
Morning will find them—
heads caved in with birth.

The Creation of Man:
The Sistine Chapel

Then I remember being drawn toward him
as my mind snapped alive
like light cast back from water

And my face, flushed, lifted
like a flower petal's muscle

But my arm and wrist remained limp
like a stem without water

As my eyes teared in the choiring wind
that became his white, streaming
hair and beard

That framed the fierce gaze
that directed the finger
that said rise

rise from the mud in my likeness.

And I half-rose toward him
out of the earth's languor
because of this
and what lay half-hidden, peering
over his far shoulder.

Oh she looked at me afraid
but with desire
like I at him.
I knew this was woman,

And in my dream looked further
toward the joy   blue   green   future
where there was a garden

Whose gate
slammed shut forever

And my face nodded down
like a rose beyond summer, autumn
and a long, long winter

Until I felt my flesh smear
like mud anew
as the pastels, their
pigments in plaster set in

And with my tattooed eyes saw
another face
not looking down but upwards —
tired, paint-streaked and mortal.

And I loved this man strapped to the scaffold,
loved him as though he were my father.

Archaeology

We have been digging for hours,
Slowly troweling the clay-red
Soil, hollowing out the darker circles
Where rotted fence posts were.
For two weeks, nothing; then

Steel tine scraping bone, its echo
And gullied sound. A show of white.
The skull like a sullen root
You trace with the pick, as though it
Were etching your hand in chalk.

With a sable brush you dust
The brow. It is thin, not thick. A female.
We flesh out the skull. A few loose
Teeth, corn-yellow seeds, their crowns
Slow frozen flowers. We work

Into evening, shallowing out
The clavicles and sternum, each rib
—like building a cage of air—
The length of both arms and shattered
Hands offer the splayed pelvis,

Its ghost ear, a lobe-petalled
Fungus, listening from earth.
The legs, femur and tibia perfectly
Intact, interred with the dusk
As we step back and gaze. We are

Volunteers, volunteered to touch
What shines like a splintered moon
Held in relief. The coin of ourselves,
Our future's past, we look down
To save and spend in a glance.

Eurydice Talking

Sometimes we make it to the landing.
I do this for you, after
all, even agony prolonged
becomes a joy,
and this is repetition.
The garish snapshot in your mind—

why am I so patient?
When you place your hand
upon the rail, I know my name
rumors light like running water

as you stray between the yes and no
then turn to flood the darkness.
What can I tell you?
Desire cannot be commanded.

Once is now, this undertow
forever. Keep turning.
It was your carelessness
that makes the song worth singing.

The Invention of the Snowman

Somewhere beyond the bounds of sleep
my bones undressed, rising from their flesh
to become this selfless, falling dust.

It was then I wanted ears
with which to hear the familiar cries
of those children building me.

And of course I had no eyes
only this unfailing bandage of light,
the snow sewing its colorless view.

But worst of all, this thirst to be living —
to understand those small, clumsy hands
making the same careless mistakes as gods.

Augustifolia

When you see on a woman's face
a bruise, pale flotsam and purpling,
you may understand the orchid —
How at first one turns away from the vulgar
only to be stricken by beauty,
for the bruise of the flesh
is moving inward.

But when the dead come to life
having slipped so many times from your heart
there will be no more healing,
for the spirit
impossibly bruised will flower
everywhere at once,
almost more weed than flower —
like lavender or augustifolia.

And this color will become the flag of a country
as personal as a sadness,
yet generous as silence or water
from which others must finally drink to listen —
And the joy will come
so far from the other side
that you will hear the sunlight on
the rust from the rain through the bells.

Church

And when all that is real
collapses, does God
shimmer on the wall like light
from a window,
the faint cameo
we touch to our cheek
as the dream
smears to precision,
the sound of stained glass
shattering, which only the mad
hear as bells?

Art

All my life
I have been drawn by its scent,
like that of an October orchard
which guides the young boy
until he stands
mesmerized before the pendulous red fruit.

And though the scent
grows stronger, still I am wandering,
afraid that when I finally arrive
I will merely discover
what is called life

where people occasionally
speak of a fleeting, yet exotic scent
called art, and a strange, but small
and seemingly purposeless
wandering tribe.

Index of Titles

Notes

"Ghost" (p. 3) and "Creation" (p. 15) in memory of Randi Schulman (1949-2007).

"Poem Beginning with a Line by Milosz" (p. 14): the line is quoted from the Czeslaw Milosz poem entitled "Hymn."

 "Rodeo" (p. 54): quotes from Sir George Peckham may be found in *The Roanoke Voyages*, 1584-1590 (London, 1955), 2 vols.

"Potter's Field" (p. 62): historic burial ground for the unidentified, many of whom were homeless and indigent, located on Hart Island, half a mile east of City Island, N.Y., N.Y.

"No Continuing City" (p. 71): the brief, fragmented quotes at the end of the poem are from John Keats' "Ode on a Grecian Urn."

"The Sheer Weight of History" (p. 89): imaginatively inspired by the painting, *The Sheer Weight of History,* Eric Fischl, 1982 (60" x 60").

"Against the Meanwhile" (p.133): these are selections from the original poem, which begins with "Point Nine" (a decimal equivalent) and ends with "Point One," nine consecutive poems in descending order.

Biographical Note

Mark Irwin was born in Faribault, Minnesota, and has lived throughout the United States and abroad in France and Italy. His poetry and essays have appeared widely in many literary magazines including *The American Poetry Review, The Atlantic, Georgia Review, The Kenyon Review, Paris Review, Poetry, The Nation, New England Review,* and the *New Republic.* He has taught at a number of universities and colleges including Case Western Reserve, the University of Iowa, Ohio University, the University of Denver, the University of Colorado/Boulder, the University of Nevada, and Colorado College. The author of seven collections of poetry, *The Halo of Desire* (1987), *Against the Meanwhile,* Wesleyan University Press (1989), *Quick, Now, Always,* BOA (1996), *White City,* BOA (2000), *Bright Hunger,* BOA (2004), *Tall If,* New Issues (2008), and *Large White House Speaking,* New Issues (2013), he has also translated two volumes of poetry, one from the French and one from the Romanian. Recognition for his work includes The Nation/Discovery Award, four Pushcart Prizes, National Endowment for the Arts and Ohio Art Council Fellowships, Colorado Council for the Arts Fellowships, two Colorado Book Awards, the James Wright Poetry Award, and fellowships from the Fulbright, Lilly, and Wurlitzer Foundations. He lives in Colorado, and Los Angeles, where he teaches in the Ph.D. in Literature & Creative Writing Program at the University of Southern California. Mark Irwin is also a member of the MFA Faculty in Creative Writing at Ashland University.